THE LITTLE BOOK OF
ST PATRICK'S DAY

Published by OH!
20 Mortimer Street
London W1T 3JW

Text © 2020 OH!
Design © 2020 OH!

ISBN 978-1-80069-000-4

Compiled by: Chas Newkey-Burden
Editorial: Victoria Godden, Katie Meegan
Design: Luke Griffin
Project manager: Russell Porter
Production: Rachel Burgess

A CIP catalogue record for this book is available from the British Library

Printed in Dubai

10 9 8 7 6 5 4 3 2 1

Illustrations: Macrovector/Freepik.com

THE LITTLE BOOK OF

ST PATRICK'S DAY

A CELEBRATION OF THE IRISH

CONTENTS

INTRODUCTION

The history of St Patrick's Day contains many surprises.

Although it has been observed since the 10th century, St Patrick's Day did not start to become the occasion we know and love until the 17th and 18th centuries. What is now regarded as an occasion to enjoy a drink or two was once a day of quiet abstinence, with bars closed across Ireland.

The story of the saint himself may also surprise you. He was not Irish, was never formally canonised as a saint and yet he became the patron saint of Ireland. Much of his story is entwined with myth and symbolism: he probably didn't drive snakes out of Ireland and some historians say that the St Patrick spoken of today is actually a composite of two people.

   None of this detail bothers revellers on the big day. Cities around the world hold parades, packed bars blast Irish music and everything seems to turn green for the day. St Patrick's Day is even observed in outer space. For one day, we are all Irish.

   From the days when drinkers attended the Dublin Dog Show because it had the only open bar in Ireland, to the 21st century, when pub profits rocket on 17 March, the day has changed a lot. Along the way, it has taught us much about Ireland, festivity and ourselves. It is the national holiday that the planet embraced.

CHAPTER
ONE

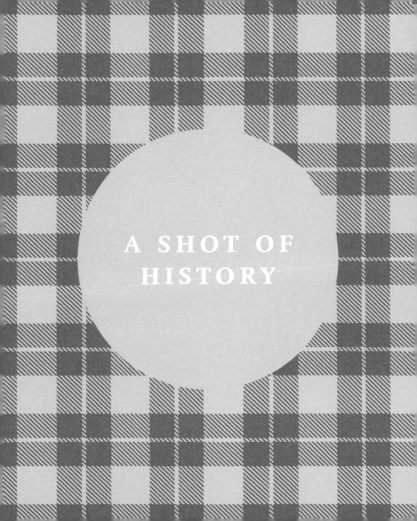

A SHOT OF
HISTORY

Once a day of abstinence from alcohol, St Patrick's Day has now become an occasion for record-breaking sales of the black stuff and other boozy beverages.

This magical festival has evolved and taught us much about the world.

"

To-morrow, being the anniversary of St Patrick, Tutelar Saint of Ireland, will be observed with the usual respect and attention, by his generous sons and their descendants.

"

Notice in Rivington's NY Gazette, 16 March 1775

Golden Nuggets

St Patrick's Day is held on
17 March because this is the
supposed date of his death.

The first St Patrick's Day festival
was held in Boston, USA in 1737.

Historians believe that St Patrick's
Day was first celebrated in
New York at the Crown & Thistle
Tavern in 1756.

A Quiet Night in

Until the 1700s, St Patrick's Day
was only observed in Ireland.

This Roman Catholic event was
usually spent reflectively, in quiet
prayer at church or at home.

Origins No.1

It is believed that the first St Patrick's Day parade was held on 17 March 1601 in a Spanish colony in what is now St Augustine, Florida, USA. There were then parades in Boston and New York in the middle of the 18th century.

In 1607 it was listed as a saint's day in the Irish legal calendar.

A 17th-century Franciscan priest,
Luke Wadding, effectively created
St Patrick's Day. Although it had been
celebrated since the 10th century,
he convinced the Catholic Church
to recognise it and turn it into a
festival proper.

Fight for Your Right

In 1768, Irish coal-heavers in London went on strike. On St Patrick's Day they marched through Wapping and Shadwell, wearing a shamrock in their hats.

During the American Revolution in 1780, George Washington granted the Continental Army a holiday "as an act of solidarity with the Irish in their fight for independence".

Irish Roots

The celebration of St Patrick's Day in America took off when the Irish potato famine hit in 1845 and large amounts of people began migrating to the United States from Ireland.

Origins No.2

In 1848, a number of New York Irish Aid societies decided to unite their parades to form one official New York City St Patrick's Day Parade.

The New York Times reports that in 1867, police were assaulted during a "St Patrick's Day Riot", during which "swords and spears [were] in use again".

In the second half of the 19th century, the elite of Irish society began to mark the day with a grand ball in Dublin Castle.

Momentous Events

Major historical events to occur on 17 March include: Julius Caesar's final victory in 45BC; Portuguese navigator Ferdinand Magellan reaching the Philippines in 1521; and British warship *Queen Charlotte* catching fire in 1800.

Golden Nuggets

According to History.com,
when Irish Americans in US cities
first took to the streets on
St Patrick's Day, newspaper
cartoons depicted them as drunk,
violent, ape-like creatures.

Although pubs were often closed
for St Patrick's Day, the Dublin
Dog Show was exempt and
therefore became the only place
where people could go for a drink.

Origins No.3

In 1948, President Harry S. Truman attended New York City's St Patrick's Day Parade. This was considered a watershed moment for the Irish American community which had previously been mocked and discriminated against.

In 1991, the United States made March the official Irish–American Heritage month, choosing March to tie in with St Patrick's Day.

The first St Patrick's Day concerts were organised by the Gaelic League in the 1890s and were staged annually at central London venues such as the Queen's Hall and Holborn Hall until the 1950s.

Lucky Birthday

Famous Irish people born on
St Patrick's Day include footballer
Pat Rice (1949), Boyzone singer
Stephen Gately (1976) and
Caroline Corr, the singer and
drummer of the folk rock band
The Corrs (1973).

Origins No.4

In 1940, the religious celebrations of St Patrick's Day were moved when the day clashed with Palm Sunday.

In 1996, the St. Patrick's Festival was first held in Dublin – a four-day event of music, treasure hunts, performances and a two-hour parade.

Sporting Rivalries

On 17 March, Celtic beat fierce rivals Rangers 2-0. Three Rangers players were sent off, leading to the match being nicknamed the St Patrick's Day Massacre. Celtic's manager said: "Maybe St Patrick was watching that afternoon and decided to give us a hand."

Across the Atlantic on the very same day, the hockey side St Louis Blues took on the Chicago Blackhawks. A brawl broke out that saw 12 players ejected (six from each team). That match also became known as the St Patrick's Day Massacre.

Golden Nuggets

The first St Patrick's Day
parade in Ireland wasn't held
until 1931.

St Patrick's Day became an
official national holiday in the US
in 1903.

Drink it Up

It wasn't until the 1960s that pubs in the Emerald Isle were allowed to open on 17 March. It had taken years of campaigning by Irish politician James O'Mara to overcome fears that such openings would promote excessive drinking.

Shamrock Splendor

In 1961, on JFK's first St Patrick's Day in the White House, Ireland's ambassador, Thomas J. Kiernan, visited the Oval Office to present the traditional ceremonial bowl of shamrock to the President. The presentation of a shamrock bowl to the US President is a tradition that has continued to this day.

Drink it Up

The association between alcohol and St Patrick's Day strengthened in the 1980s when there was a huge marketing push tied into the festival from the American beer Budweiser.

Paddy Time

In 2002, the Greater London Authority started holding a new St. Patrick's Day parade and festival in Trafalgar Square. By 2015, it was attracting average crowds of 125,000.

Party Postponed

In 2001, foot and mouth disease delayed the official celebration in Dublin for over two months. It was eventually held on 21 May.

The St Patrick's Day parade was cancelled outright in Dublin and elsewhere in the country in 2020 due to the COVID-19 pandemic.

Drink it Up

On an average day, 5.5 million pints of Guinness are consumed around the world, but on St Patrick's Day, that number more than doubles to 13 million pints, according to the drinks company.

Paddy Time

According to a survey in 2014, 97 per cent of Americans planned to celebrate the holiday in one form or another, with 41 per cent of Americans spending the night out with friends at a bar or party and 30 per cent celebrating with family.

Golden Nuggets

Dingle, in County Kerry, holds
the honour of the earliest
St Patrick's Day parade – it gets
underway at 6am!

Dripsey, County Cork used to
hold the shortest St Patrick's Day
parade. It has since been replaced
by the annual Dripsey Vintage
Tractor and Car Run!

Drink it Up

In 2000, a major debate was held in Ireland over whether bubbles move up or down when you pour Guinness into a glass.

In 2012, a group of Irish mathematicians proved that the nitrogen bubbles in the stout react to the shape of the glass, which drags the bubbles downward. Which is why it's so important to drink from a Guinness glass!

Airtime

On St Patrick's Day 2019, the Alan Patridge comedy series *This Time* featured Steve Coogan as an Irish farmer singing rebel songs on the BBC show.

In 2020, the BBC tea-time quiz series *Pointless Celebrities* broadcast an Ireland special episode on 17 March, featuring Irish guests Mick Foster, Tony Allen, Pauline McLynn, Vogue Williams, Clodagh McKenna, Anna Haugh, Henry Kelly and Jimmy Cricket.

CHAPTER
TWO

WE NEED TO
TALK ABOUT
PATRICK

He wasn't Irish and was never canonised as a saint.

So how did he become the patron saint of Ireland?

Patrick's life story is full of drama.

Golden Nuggets

The man who became the patron saint of Ireland is said to have been born in either Scotland or Wales in 386AD.

St Patrick is said to have combined the sun with the Christian cross to make the Celtic cross.

St Patrick used the Shamrock, growing wildly in ditches, to represent the Holy Trinity and convert the pagans of Ireland to Christianity.

Who is Patrick?

Saint Patrick wasn't short of monikers. In his own writings, he refers to himself as Patricius, but in other works he is named Magonus, Succetus and Cothirthiacus.

According to legend, St Patrick's real birth name was actually Maewyn Succat; he changed his name to Patricius, or Patrick, which derives from the Latin term for "father figure", when he became a priest.

Spiritual Story No.1

Canonisation in the Roman Catholic Church was not introduced until after Patrick's death in the 5th century, so he was never canonised by the Catholic Church.

This means he is not a saint by the standards accepted today but is widely considered a saint in heaven.

Chapter and Verse

St Patrick wrote an autobiography called *Confessio* (or *Confession*).

In it, he writes that when he was about 16 years of age, he was captured by Irish pirates from his home in Britain and taken as a slave to Ireland.

He says that his time in captivity helped his spiritual development.

Spiritual Story No.2

He eventually escaped to France, where he became a monk, but by about 432 he had become a bishop and returned to Ireland as a missionary.

It wasn't the smoothest of returns. Soon after he arrived, he met the chieftan of one of the druid tribes, who tried to kill him.

He was imprisoned several times by local pagan chiefs. To try to placate them, Patrick would sometimes offer them gifts.

On one occasion he tried to escape from Ireland, stowing away on a boat bound for Britain.

Who is Patrick?

After he arrived in Ireland, he spent six years herding sheep and pigs on Slemish mountain in County Antrim. He spent most of his spare time praying.

"

I am the sinner Patrick. I am the most unsophisticated of people, the least of Christians, and for many people I am the most contemptible.

"

St Patrick

Writing in his book The Confession

Golden Nuggets

As a missionary, he baptised
many thousands of people.

He ultimately preached in Ireland
for 40 years, converting the
people and building churches
across the country.

Who is Patrick?

St Patrick carried a walking stick
made of wood from an ash tree.
When he stopped to preach, he
would push the walking stick
into the ground.

One day, he preached for so
long that it is said the stick
developed roots and turned into
a living tree.

Spiritual Story No.3

Although Patrick was the primary patron saint of Ireland, the country has two other patron saints: Saint Brigit of Kildare, whose feast day is held on 1 February, and Saint Colmcille, who is thought to have written *The Book of Kells*, who is celebrated on 9 June.

> ❝
> The love of God and his fear grew in me more and more, as did the faith, and my soul was rosed, so that, in a single day, I have said as many as a hundred prayers and in the night, nearly the same.
> I prayed in the woods and on the mountain, even before dawn. I felt no hurt from the snow or ice or rain.
> ❞

St Patrick
Writing in his book The Confession

Spiritual Story No.4

It is believed that in 431AD, Pope Celestine sent a bishop known as Palladius "to the Irish believing in Christ".

Some believe that St Patrick is actually an amalgam of two men: Palladius and the deacon's son who first visited Ireland as a slave.

On a Mission

Patrick believed that once "every nation" had heard the gospel, Christ would return. He regarded Ireland as the "final hurdle" of God's plan.

66

Patrick is a saint by
acclamation and not a saint
by act of a pope. He was
an apostle to Ireland and
universally recognized as so.

99

Gordon Robertson
Executive producer of the movie I Am Patrick
as seen on crosswalk.com

Golden Nuggets

It is believed that St Patrick was
not keen on eating meat and
instead enjoyed a diet of oats,
seaweed, vegetables and nuts.

It is widely believed that
St Patrick was the first to claim
that the shamrock can be a good
luck charm.

Slithering Tale

Legend has it that St Patrick stood atop an Irish hillside and banished snakes from Ireland. It is said that the serpents slithered into the sea.

However, research suggests snakes never lived in the Emerald Isle in the first place as there are no signs of snakes in the country's fossil record as the snakes were too slow to make it across the land bridges of the ice age.

"

Patrick was really a first –
the first missionary to
barbarians beyond the reach
of Roman law. The step he
took was in its way as bold as
Columbus's, and a thousand
times more humane.

"

Thomas Cahill
Writing in his book
How the Irish Saved Civilization

66

He was fearless and he gave of himself unselfishly. That's why the Irish love him.

99

Reverend Michael Roach
Pastor at St Bartholomew in Manchester as seen on
BaltimoreMagazine.com.

Spiritual Story No.5

Just as much of Patrick's life is
shrouded with mystery, so is his
death. He is widely believed to
be buried at Down Cathedral
in Downpatrick, County Down,
alongside Saint Brigid and
Saint Colmcille.

> 66
>
> God watched over me before
> I knew him, and before
> I learned sense or even
> distinguished between good
> and evil, and he protected
> me, and consoled me as a
> father would his son
>
> 99

St Patrick
As seen on GoodReads.com

Seat of Judgement

According to legend,
on the Day of Judgement, while
Jesus Christ judges all other
nations, St Patrick will be the
judge of the Irish.

CHAPTER
THREE

MAGIC AND MYTHS

From lucky clovers to snake races and cabbage fights, St Patrick's Day is a day of fun and frolics.

Read on to discover the mystic origins of everyone's favourite party.

Golden Nuggets

In Gaelic, the shamrock's name
is "seamróg", which means
summer plant.

The four-leafed clover has been
part of Irish culture dating from
as far back as the ancient Druids,
who believed that the plant
held "special powers to combat
evil spirits".

Drink it Up

Guinness is served 819% more often on St Patrick's Day than any other day of the year.

Golden Nuggets

The US army raised a few eyebrows in 2018 when it published a video celebrating St Patrick's Day that featured a helicopter firing shamrock missiles.

All shamrocks are clovers but not all clovers are shamrocks. Clovers can be found all over northern Europe but the shamrock is only native to Ireland.

Festival of Food

Cabbage shipments in the US increase 70% in the week leading up to the big day. Corned beef and cabbage has become a favourite across Ireland on St Patrick's Day, but it originated in America. Back in Ireland, people ate ham and cabbage, but for impoverished Irish immigrants in the US, corned beef was a cheaper substitute.

Golden Nuggets

According to legend, each leaf
of a four-leafed clover has
a meaning: Hope, Faith, Love
and Luck.

Your odds of finding a four-leaf
clover are about 1 in 10,000.

Leprechaun Lore

One St Patrick's Day myth states that if you hurt a leprechaun the devil will tie you with chains and curse you.

Green is the Colour

Although green is the colour of
St Patrick's Day, knights in the
Order of St Patrick actually wore
a colour known as St Patrick's
blue. It is believed the colour
changed in the 18th century,
when Irish rebels adopted green
as their colour.

Golden Nuggets

The wearing of green is
also said to represent the coming
of spring.

San Francisco has held snake-
racing events on St Patrick's Day.

Big Spenders

A study by Wallethub estimated that $6.16 billion is spent in the name of the Emerald Isle each year. This means the average person spends $40 during their celebrations.

Fairy Tale

The leprechaun is a common icon of St Patrick's Day celebrations. Some say their place in folklore seems to have stemmed from Celtic belief in fairies. However, a recent study concluded that the word "leprechaun" originated in Ancient Rome – meaning the name of a Roman god in charge of protecting flocks and his cheeky male followers.

On This Day

Other observances falling on
17 March include Children's Day
in Bangladesh, Evacuation Day in
Suffolk County, Massachusetts,
and the feast day of Gertrude
of Nivelles.

Irish America

St Patrick's Day has become a big deal in the US partly due to the sheer force of numbers: the population of Irish Americans is seven times the population of Ireland.

There are 193 cities in America with an Irish population of 10% or more.

Relations Reunited

The celebration often brings
relatives together. It did that to
spectacular effect when an
Irish policeman came face to face
with his American cop cousin
for the first time in 40 years
at the St Patrick's Day parade in
New York in 2019.

Éire Episodes

Several popular comedies and dramas have recorded episodes themed around St Patrick's Day.

On *Cheers*, characters were forced to strip naked as a forfeit; on *How I Met Your Mother*, Ted wakes up in a bin; and in *Sabrina the Teenage Witch*, Sabrina is granted three wishes by a leprechaun.

Feature Film

The life of St Patrick was told
in an historical drama on
Netflix, entitled *I am Patrick:
The Patron Saint of Ireland.*

Tree-rific

In recent years, St Patrick's Day trees have become part of the celebrations for some Americans. Based on Christmas trees, they are topped with either a giant shamrock or a leprechaun hat.

Irish Celebrities

Terry Wogan was voted the coolest Irish celebrity in a poll of the British public to mark St Patrick's Day.

The 2010 survey saw the broadcaster beat off stiff competition from actor Pierce Brosnan, presenter Christine Bleakley and… X *Factor* contestants Jedward.

Irish Rover

In 2010, The Dubliners' rendition of "The Irish Rover" was voted the most popular song with which to celebrate St Patrick's Day.

Other acts attracting votes in the poll included U2, Johnny Cash and Thin Lizzy.

Top Irish Exports

However, in a 2020 poll,
St Patrick's Day was voted only
the 10th best thing to ever come
out of Ireland. This put it behind
Father Ted, George Best, and
Riverdance, but above Westlife
and Ryanair.

Social Media Faux Pas

The paternal grandparents of former England international Wayne Rooney are Irish, but the footballer was left red-faced when he posted a St Patrick's Day message on Instagram, accidentally using an emoji of the Ivory Coast flag.

It was even more awkward in 2018 when none other than the Irish Taoiseach (Prime Minister) Leo Varadkar made the same error on Twitter.

In 2016, the OECD think tank apologised after using St Patrick's Day to launch new statistics on alcohol abuse, complete with a green, white and orange chart on Twitter. After an outcry, the company deleted the post and said: "It's not a tweet that we were proud of."

The same year, Lewisham Police also caused offence when the force tweeted an image of two pairs of handcuffs, shaped as a four-leafed clover. Following complaints that the image stereotyped the Irish as criminals, the tweet was removed.

Shamrock Record

The world record for the largest human shamrock was broken by hundreds of green-clad revellers in the US on St Patrick's Day 2019.

A grand total of 1,200 people gathered in the city of Elmira, New York for the occasion. The previous record saw an 851-person human shamrock set by students in Dublin.

Flying the Flag

Sales of Irish flags also soar in the run-up to the big day. Worldwide Flags, a West Scotland-based family business, told the *Telegraph* that his company sells "easily 10 times as many Irish flags as normal".

Shamrock Gift

Since the 1950s, Irish government leaders have presented the US President with a bowl of shamrocks at the White House on St Patrick's Day. According to CNN, "any food, drink or plant presented to the President has to be handled pursuant to Secret Service policy" – or, in other words, destroyed.

Green Jerseys

The Toronto Maple Leafs in the National Hockey League of Canada were known as Toronto St Patrick's from 1919 to 1927 and wore green jerseys.

In 1999, when they had a broadcast game on St Patrick's night, they wore green again.

Change the Date

In 2017, the Russian Orthodox Church recognised the day for the first time but it held the commemoration on 30 March.

Irish Tricolour

The Irish flag was initially banned from St Patrick's Day celebrations in Northern Ireland in 2018. However, amid talk on an unofficial breakaway parade, Derry City and Strabane District Council backed down and allowed the famous tricolour.

Shamrock Shake

The fast food chain McDonald's
sells McDonald's Shamrock
Shakes in Ireland during
the St Patrick's Day season.
The mint- flavoured shakes
are a garish green colour and
surprisingly delicious.

Teddy Bear's Picnic

In many houses across Ireland
in 2020, families had teddy bears
as guests in their homes on
St Patrick's Day, in place of
human guests who were not
allowed to visit because of
coronavirus restrictions.

Make America Green

In 2020, US President Donald Trump refused to attend the annual St Patrick's Day lunch on Capitol Hill because the host, the Speaker Nancy Pelosi, "has chosen to tear this Nation apart with her actions and her rhetoric".

However, Trump did get into the spirit of it in 2017, when he launched green MAGA (Make America Great Again) baseball caps on the big day.

Later on that same day, the
US President put his foot in it when
he recited a proverb to mark the
occasion. However, it was pointed
out that the proverb was not actually
Irish and was probably a passage
from a Nigerian poem.

CHAPTER
FOUR

HOW TO
CELEBRATE

There are many ways to celebrate St Patrick's Day. Here is your guide to what to drink, what to eat and what to wear.

You can also discover some fun traditions, including drowning the shamrock.

Emerald Green

Drink green beer.

This Irish American drink can be
found across bars on the big day...
or you can make your own.
Simply add a few drops of green
food dye to a pint of beer.
The more dye you add, the more
it will turn your teeth green.

Golden Nuggets

Parents can make green
chocolate chip cookies for their
children.

Say "Éire go Brách"
(pronounced "Erin go Bragh")
which means
"Ireland forever"!

Emerald Green

Pinch someone.

It is believed that this tradition
revolves around the leprechaun
and the legend that wearing
green makes one invisible to the
impish fairies.

Emerald Green

If you want to say
"Happy St Patrick's Day" in
Irish then say
"Lá fhéile Pádraig sona dhuit!"

Pronounce it:
"Lah Faye-la PAW-drig SUN-uh
Ditch."

Irish Modernism

Listen to Irish poetry.

The Emerald Isle is one of the most poetic nations, so why not head online and listen to the works of the likes of W. B. Yeats, Seamus Heaney and Samuel Beckett.

66

Ireland is a land of poets
and legends, of dreamers
and rebels.

99

Nora Roberts

66

St Patrick's Day is an
enchanted time – a day to
begin transforming
winter's dreams into
summer's magic.

99

Adrienne Cook

Festival of Food

There are numerous dishes from the Emerald Isle worth your consideration. These include Irish boxty (a potato pancake) and the Dublin coddle – a mixture of potatoes, sausage and onions topped with bacon.

Shepherd's pie is another popular St Patrick's Day meal.

Literary Greats

Read an Irish book.

Classic Irish novels include James Joyce's *Dubliners* and *Finnegan's Wake*, *The Country Girls* by Edna O'Brien, and *Angela's Ashes* by Frank McCourt.

The Big Screen

Watch Irish-themed films.

Relax and enjoy an evening in with films like *Brooklyn, Once, My Left Foot* and *The Wind That Shook The Barley*.

The True Spirt

While some people toast
St Patrick's Day with a drink or
two, an alternative option is to
join the Sober St Patrick's Day
movement, which aims to "reclaim
the true spirit of St Patrick's Day
by changing the perception and
experience from an occasion for
binge drinking and other misuse
of alcohol to a celebration of the
richness of Irish culture and the
legacy of St Patrick".

Holy Trinty

Go to a church.

Many have a special service for St Patrick on 17 March.

In Ireland, it is a holy day of obligation, meaning that believers are expected to attend mass. Many masses in the country are also said in Gaelic to mark the occassion.

108

The Sounds of Ireland

Listen to Irish music.

Your playlist could include The Pogues, The Wolfetones, U2, The Cranberries, Flogging Molly, The Dubliners and Christy Moore.

Festival of Food

Bake some Irish soda bread.

This is easy because the recipe uses baking soda instead of yeast and therefore the loaf doesn't need time for rising. When it's ready, why not spread some Irish butter on it?

Drink it Up

There is also a shamrock-infused
gin, with all the ingredients
sourced in County Louth.

Festival of Food

Vegans have their own plant-based festive snack – green Irish soda bread, using spinach to get the green colouring.

66

A good friend is like a four-leaf clover, hard to find and lucky to have.

99

Irish proverb

Drink it Up

A tradition known as "drowning the shamrock" sees revellers make a toast to St Patrick then toss a shamrock over the shoulder for good luck.

Paddy Time

If you have to work in an office on the big day, you can still mark the occasion. Why not wear a shamrock tie?

Golden Nuggets

Paint your face with shamrocks
or the colours of the Irish flag:
green, white and orange.

In parts of the northeast
of the US, some celebrate by
planting peas.

The Blarney Bunch

Kissing the Blarney Stone
shouldn't only be done for luck –
mythology says that it also makes
you more eloquent, giving you
"the gift of the gab".

Lucky Cake

A fun Irish Halloween tradition that can also be brought into your St Patrick Day festivities is the Barmbrack (bairín breac) cake. Made with cold tea, whiskey and dried fruit, this traditional Celtic teacake has an extra edge of fun. It is tradition to place items such as a pea, a stick, a piece of cloth, a small coin and a ring into the cake batter. Whatever item turns up in your slice symbolises your fortune for the year ahead. The best things to get are the coin and the ring, which foretell marriage and prosperity.

The Pilgrims' Walk

You could follow St Patrick's Trail in Northern Ireland, which includes Armagh's two impressive cathedrals dedicated to the saint.

Drink it Up

If you can get hold of a bottle, why not try the Foreign Extra Stout version of Guinness that is sold in Nigeria?

Be careful – it has an alcohol content of 7.5 per cent, compared to the 4 per cent version in standard Guinness.

What's the Craic?

Try out some Irish lingo. If
someone asks you how you are,
you can reply: "I'm grand." If you
want to tell someone they're an
idiot, tell them they're an "eejit".

Golden Nuggets

Put your stockings on
inside-out – Irish folklore says
this will make you lucky.

Wear a "Kiss me I'm Irish" t-shirt
and enjoy the smooches.

Céilí Community

In the run-up to St Patrick's Day you could learn a few Irish dance moves.

Check out classes on YouTube for céilí dancing and impress your friends on the day!

CHAPTER
FIVE

GLOBAL
GAELIC GAIETY

St Patrick's Day was once only marked in Ireland.

It is now observed around the planet and beyond.

Whether you are in the Middle East, Africa or outer space, someone will be celebrating the big day.

Space Flute

On St Patrick's Day 2011, the Irish-American astronaut Catherine Coleman played a 100-year-old flute belonging to the Irish band The Chieftains, while floating weightless in the space station.

Her performance was later included in a track called "The Chieftains in Orbit".

Public Holiday

As well as being a public holiday in the Republic of Ireland and Northern Ireland, St Patrick's Day is also one in the Canadian province of Newfoundland and Labrador (for provincial government employees), and the British Overseas Territory of Montserrat.

Drink it Up

St Patrick's Day is the fourth most popular drinking day in America behind New Year's Eve, Christmas, and the Fourth of July.

Around the World

In Israel, revellers gather at Molly Bloom's, the very first Irish pub to open up in the Holy Land, to celebrate.

A local history club in Banwen, Wales stages a parade that leads to a stone commemorating where they say the patron saint of Ireland was born.

In Brisbane, Australia, the
Queensland Irish Association
parade celebrates Australia's
immigrant history alongside St
Patrick's Day. Aussies dress up as
people sent to build a nation.

Hawaii holds an annual St
Patrick's Day parade, followed by
an Emerald Ball. There is a hula
song about an Irish-Hawaiian
named Lola O'Brien.

66

May the best day of your
past be the worst day of your
future.

99

Irish blessing

66

May the road rise up to meet you. May the wind be always at your back.

99

Irish blessing

Emerald Green

Since 1962, the city of Chicago has been dyeing its main river green to mark St Patrick's Day.

In 2020, the city called off all the celebrations because of the Covid-19 pandemic.

However, the North Branch of the waterway did still turn green. No one knows who the culprit was but some have speculated it was leprechauns.

Spending the Greens

On St Patrick's Day 2018,
Americans spent a record-
breaking $5.9 billion at bars,
with the average person
splashing out $39.65.

Around the World

In Accra, Ghana, a relaxing ocean retreat has held a St Patrick's Day celebration, including an Irish-themed menu with wonders such as a "grilled boozy beef steak marinated in whiskey" served with potato salad.

St Patrick is also the patron saint of Nigeria. The African nation is the second largest stout market in the world by net value ahead of both Ireland and the US.

The city of Boston, where many Irish immigrants settled once they arrived in America, hosts one of the longest parades in the US. It is usually about three miles long.

Emerald Green

In 2018, new landmarks turned green for St Patrick's Day, including the Great Wall of China, the Venetian Hotel in Las Vegas and the Palestinian Museum in Ramallah.

Short Parade

Between 1999 and 2007, the Irish village of Dripsey held the shortest St Patrick's Day parade in the world. The route ran for 78 feet between two pubs.

Since then, Hot Springs, Arkansas holds the record for the shortest parade – a mere 98 feet.

Drink it Up

In the UK, the busiest Irish-themed O'Neill's pubs get through up to 16 barrels of Guinness in just one day – the normal daily rate is just half a barrel.

Out of this World

On St Patrick's day in 2020, the International Space Station's Twitter account shared photographs taken by astronauts of green auroras seen from orbit, and views of Ireland taken 400 kilometres (250 miles) above.

Irish Guards

In 2018, Kate Middleton celebrated with the Irish Guards on St Patrick's Day. She presented an Irish Wolf Hound with a bunch of shamrocks.

Emerald Green

Green dye is added to the
fountain in front of the White
House to give the water a
St Patrick's Day hue.

Around the World

Tokyo held its first St Patrick's Day parade in 1992, and it has only grown bigger. It has become a popular event, with a blend of Irish and Japanese costumes.

In India, St Patrick's Day comes soon after the nation's Holi festival, so there is already festivity in the air when the Gateway of India is turned green on the big day.

Dublin Cities

The capital of Ireland is not the only place named Dublin to hold St Patrick's Day celebrations – there are 16 cities named Dublin across the US.

66

May the lilt of Irish laughter
lighten every load.
May the mist of Irish magic
shorten every road.

99

Irish blessing

66

The heart of an Irishman is
nothing but his imagination.

99

George Bernard Shaw
The Irish playwright

Around the World

In Brussels, a landmark statue in the city centre called Manneken Pis wears a cable-knit sweater for the occasion.

A Texan town has a proud history of celebrating the day since 1938. It takes it so seriously it even has a four-day event. Well it might – the town's name is Shamrock.

The Wisconsin town of New London changes its name to 'New Dublin' for its week-long St Patrick's Day festivities.

In O'Neill in Nebraska, the world's largest shamrock is painted in the middle of a road. Its St Patrick's Day celebrations include a hypnotist and fish fry.

66

For each petal on the shamrock, this brings a wish your way: Good health, good luck, and happiness for today and every day.

99

Irish blessing

I wish that I could stop
feeling that I want to be an
Irish girl in Ireland.

*Eilis Lacey (played by Saoirse Ronan)
in the movie* Brooklyn

Around the World

In Italy, tens of thousands of people descend on the historic university town of Padua, just a short drive from Treviso, to have a party at Festa Irlandese.

In Seattle, parade routes are painted in green. Revellers are supposed to wear green or else risk being pinched.

The people of Vilnius, in Lithuania, celebrate St Patrick's Day by turning the Vilnele River green!

In New Zealand, a parade is held in Auckland during the day, and the Auckland Sky Tower is illuminated with green light during the night.

The Irish Village in Dubai sees a three-day celebration including dancers and live music to get people into the Irish spirit, if not the Irish spirits.

66

You gotta try your luck at
least once a day, because you
could be going around lucky
all day and not even know it.

99

Jimmy Dean
Country music singer

66

If you're Irish, it doesn't matter where you go – you'll find family.

99

Victoria Smurfit
The Irish actress

Around the World

Iceland also turns its major landmarks green, including the Harpa Concert Hall, the Pearl and Hallgrímskirkja.

The festival is marked in Saudi Arabia but is known as Ireland's National Day, to avoid a culturally jarring reference to "saints".

In Portland, Maine, some
St Patrick's Day observers plunge
into the icy-cold waters of the
Atlantic Ocean at 5:30am. They
then retire to a local restaurant
for an Irish breakfast.

In New Orleans, Louisiana, there
is a cabbage food fight, to signify
how cabbage replaced potatoes
during the potato famine.

66

May your pockets be heavy
and your heart be light, may
good luck pursue you each
morning and night.

99

Irish blessing

66

Never iron a four-leaf clover
because you don't want to
press your luck.

99

Unknown

Festival of Food

Over 30% of Americans
celebrate St Patrick's Day by
preparing a traditional
Irish meal.

Emerald Green

There used to be 100 pounds
of green dye tipped into the
Chicago river, but for
environmental reasons the
quantity has reduced to 40.

66

We may have bad weather in
Ireland, but the sun shines in
the hearts of the people and
that keeps us all warm.

99

Marianne Williamson
The American author

You've got to think lucky.
If you fall into a mudhole,
check your back pocket – you
might have caught a fish.

Darrell Royal
The American football player and coach

CHAPTER
SIX

HAVING
THE CRAIC

The Irish (and their admirers)
love a chat, a laugh and a toast.

Their sayings, jokes and quips
about St Patrick's Day never
fail to cheer.

66

For the whole world is Irish
on the Seventeenth o' March!

99

Thomas Augustine Daly
The Irish-American poet

> **"**
>
> There's an Isle, a green Isle,
> set in the sea, Here's to the
> Saint that blessed it!
>
> **"**

Jean Bleweet
From poem St Patrick's Day, *as seen on*
PoetryFoundation.org

Knock, knock

Who's there?

Irish

Irish who?

Irish you a happy
St Patrick's Day

66

The Irish folks were disappointed that the parliament did not meet today, because it was St Patrick's Day, and the mall was so full of crosses, that I thought all the world was Irish.

99

Jonathan Swift
Recalling a visit to London in 1713

“
May the roof above us never
fall in and may we friends
beneath it never fall out.
”

A popular St Patrick's Day toast

66

When Patrick drives the snakes out of Ireland, it is symbolically saying he drove the old, evil, pagan ways out of the country and brought in a new age.

99

Philip Freeman

American classics professor, as seen on OnThisDay.com

66

St Patrick… one of the
few saints whose feast day
presents the opportunity
to get determinedly whacked
and make a fool of oneself
all under the guise of
acting Irish.

99

Charles M. Madigan
As seen on Bustle.com

66

I, too, am a lover of
St Patrick's Day.

99

George Washington

“

It's the closest thing
in America to National
Immigrant Day, a tribute not
only to the Irish, but to the
idea that Americans are all
part 'other'.

”

Time *magazine puts America's relationship
with the festival in context*

66

St Patrick's Day is basically
an invention of this Irish
American contingent... Modern
celebrations really have very
little to do with Irish traditions,
or St Patrick himself.

99

Philip Freeman
American classics professor, as seen on OnThisDay.com

"

There isn't a sinner in Ireland
that would refer to a Patrick as
'Patty'. It's as simple as that.

"

Marcus Campbell
The man behind the "Paddy not Patty" campaign,
as seen on independent.co.uk

" Sláinte! "

The traditional toast when raising a glass.

66

Yeah, it's St Paddy's Day.
Everyone's Irish tonight.

99

Murphy MacManus (played by Norman Reedus) in the movie The Boondock Saints

What do you
call a fake Irish stone?

A shamrock!

A St Patrick's Day joke

180

66

The list of Irish saints is
past counting; but in it all
no other figure is so human,
friendly, and lovable as
St Patrick.

99

Stephen Gwynn
As seen on Newsweek.com

181

66

That's what the holidays are for — for one person to tell the stories and another to dispute them. Isn't that the Irish way?

99

Lara Flynn Boyle
As seen on Bustle.com

66

Anyone acquainted with
Ireland knows that the
morning of St Patrick's
Day consists of the night of
the seventeenth of March
flavoured strongly with the
morning of the eighteenth.

99

Unknown

"

It ain't over till it's clover!

"

As seen on countryliving.com

66

Today's children will tell their own children and grandchildren about the national holiday in 2020 that had no parades or parties, but instead saw everyone staying at home to protect each other.

99

Leo Varadkar

The Taoiseach (Prime Minister) of Ireland delivers a special St Patrick's Day address amid the coronavirus pandemic of 2020

185

66

The modern celebration of St Patrick's Day really has almost nothing to do with the real man.

99

Philip Freeman
American classics professor, as seen on
NationalGeographic.com

186

"

Drinking green beer doesn't make you Irish, it just makes you pee.

"

Reverend Jack Ward
A Baltimore Irish-American priest, as seen on
BaltimoreMagazine.com

66

I think it's the greatest
load of ponce.

99

An elderly Dublin man, interviewed on Ireland's
Midday programme, when asked what he thought
about St Patrick's Day

66

St Patrick's Day is a day to
celebrate our green heritage.
The ancestry of Ireland.
It is a day to celebrate what it
means to be Irish and of Irish
descent.

99

Anthony T. Hicks

66

Being Irish is very much
a part of who I am. I take it
everywhere with me.

99

Colin Farrell
The Irish actor

"

May your blessings
outnumber the shamrocks
that grow.
And may trouble avoid you
wherever you go.

"

Irish blessing

66

May your troubles be less.
And your blessings be more.
And nothing but happiness
come through your door.

99

Irish blessing